SPACE SAILING

SPACE SAILING

by D. M. Souza

 Lerner Publications Company · Minneapolis

LIBRARY OF CONGRESS CATALOGING-IN-PUBLICATION DATA

Souza, D. M. (Dorothy M.)
  Space Sailing / D.M. Souza
    p.   cm.
  Includes bibliographical references and index.
  Summary: Discusses how sunlight can be used to propel
spacecraft equipped with sails to reach destinations now
beyond the reach of conventional craft.
  ISBN 0-8225-2850-9
  1. Solar sails—Juvenile literature. 2. Space flight—
Juvenile literature. [1. Solar sails. 2. Space flight.
3. Outer space—Exploration.]
I. Title.
TL783.9.S68   1993
629.47'54—dc20   92-45176
                                            CIP
                                             AC

Manufactured in the United States of America

1 2 3 4 5 6 – I/JR – 99 98 97 96 95 94

Contents

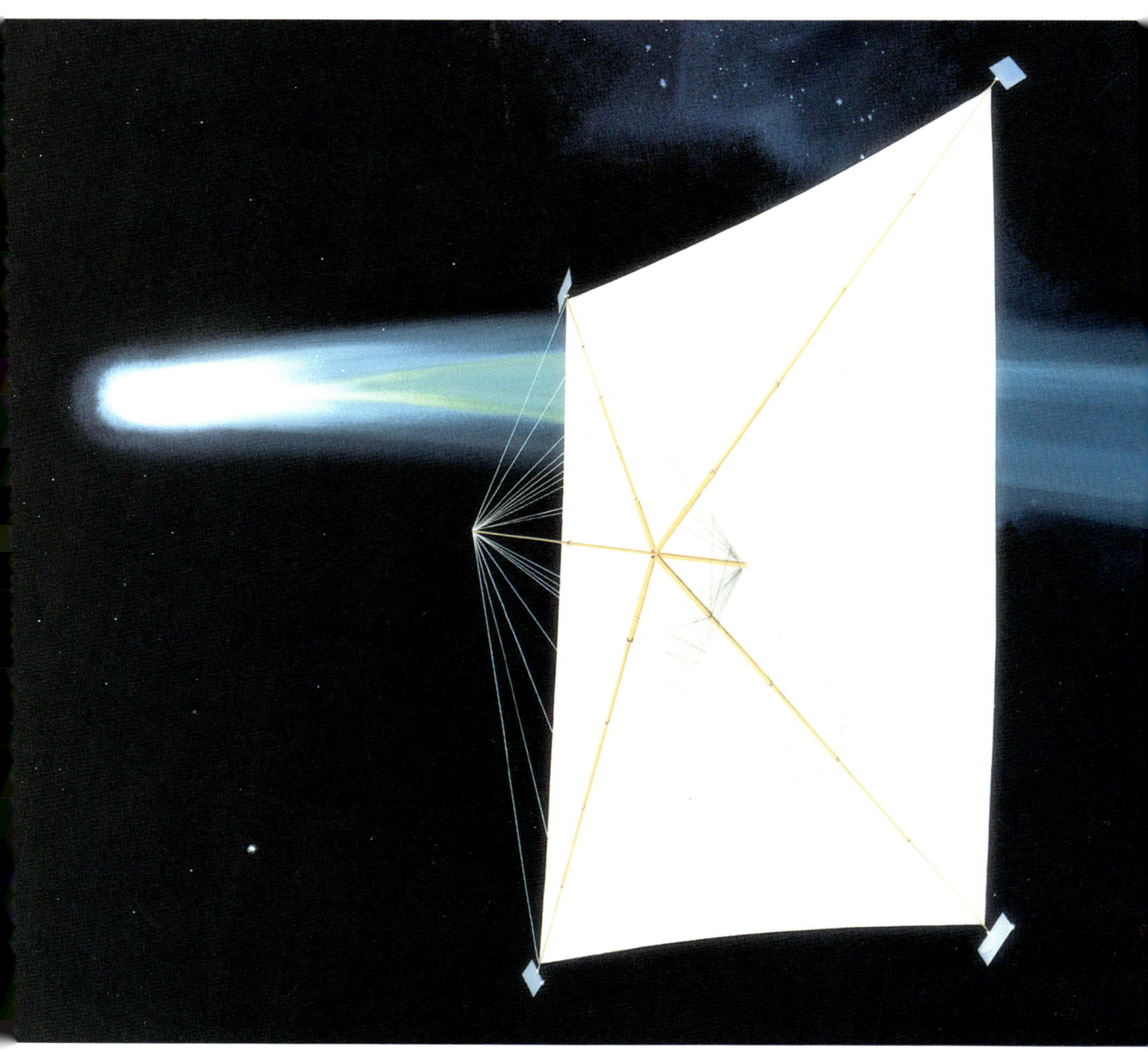

This artist's rendering shows a square sail in rendezvous with Halley's comet.

1

A Push from the Sun

She dwindled away from him, sail glittering splendidly in the sunlight that would be hers for centuries to come... She would gain two thousand miles an hour in every day of sailing. In a month, she would be traveling faster than any ship that man had ever built.
—Arthur C. Clarke

Arthur C. Clarke's short story "Wind from the Sun" vividly describes seven space sailors racing to the Moon aboard giant sailing ships propelled only by sunlight. When the story first appeared in 1964, it became a popular piece of science fiction. Many readers never imagined that such spacecraft could ever be built.

Yet yesterday's fiction is becoming today's reality. In the 1990s, scientists are learning to design space sails that can help propel a craft to other planets. And, in Japan, Europe, and the United States, scientists are actually assembling giant sails for a race to the Moon.

More than 5,000 years ago, humans first discovered that using sheets of cloth to catch the wind enabled them to move ships across the seas. Sailing ships dramatically changed people's lives. Navigators learned how to use wind-filled sails to transport people and cargo to destinations they might otherwise have never reached.

By using huge sails made of thin plastic coated with aluminum, modern-day scientists hope to send spaceships to strange places millions of miles beyond the Earth. They are convinced such spaceships will one day carry supplies, equipment, and perhaps even people to distant planets, asteroids, and even other star systems.

Scientists are planning to use the Sun's light to propel spacecraft. The movements of air that we call winds do not exist in space. While there are "solar winds" (streams of electrically charged particles called ions that radiate from the Sun), these "winds" are not involved in space sailing.

Inside the Sun

The Sun is not a solid object like the Earth, nor does it burn the way fire does. Large enough to hold a million Earths, the Sun is a huge ball of extremely hot gases. A gas is a form of matter that is neither liquid nor solid and that tends to expand. Temperatures at the Sun's core reach an estimated 27 million degrees Fahrenheit (15 million degrees Celsius). The Sun's heat and light are produced in this core.

The most abundant gas in the Sun is hydrogen. The intense heat and pres-

Space sails will be steered by sunlight much as sailboats are steered by the wind.

sure at the Sun's core cause the hydrogen atoms (the tiny particles that make up hydrogen) to break apart. The atoms then reunite to form a gas called helium. Deep inside the Sun, millions of tons of hydrogen change into helium each second. This process is known as **fusion**, and it produces tremendous amounts of energy. When this energy reaches the surface of the Sun, it radiates through space as heat and light, traveling at 186,300 miles (299,800 kilometers) per second.

Photons Provide the Push

Light is made up of particles of energy called **photons**. When they

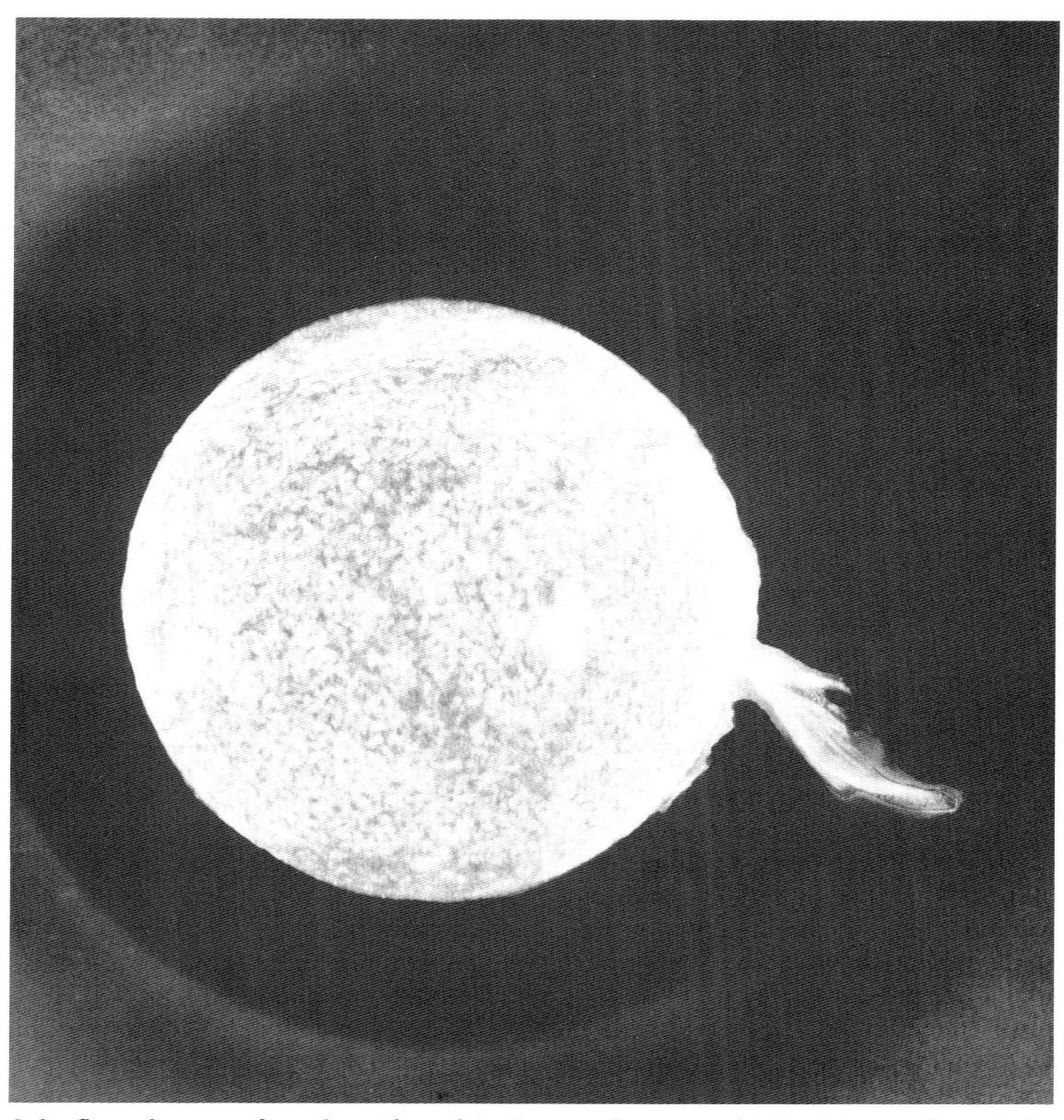

Solar flares that erupt from the surface of the Sun may be spectacular, but it is actually sunlight that will propel space sails.

strike an object, they give it a push. This push from photons is so slight it can hardly be detected on Earth. Against your hand, for example, the push from sunlight is a thousand times lighter than the weight of a feather. But in the **vacuum** of space, which contains no air or other gases, photon pressure can actually move objects.

Russian physicist Peter Lebedew (1866–1912) proved that photons exert a force. Early in this century, he experimented with photon pressure using a vacuum chamber in which air currents could not affect his findings. He flashed an intense beam of light onto a metal disk inside the chamber. The photons moved the disk, and Lebedew was able to calculate their force.

The amount of force depends on the surface of the object the photons hit. A shiny surface reflects more light than a dark, rough surface. A less reflective surface absorbs light and also absorbs some of the pressure from the impact of the photons. Therefore, the more photons a surface is able to reflect, the more force will be exerted on that surface.

Even though scientists were aware that light exerted pressure, it was not until the 20th century that the idea was applied to space travel. Konstantin Tsiolkovsky (1857–1935), a Russian schoolteacher, spent much of his spare time studying mathematics and physics,

reading the futuristic novels of Jules Verne, and dreaming of travel beyond the Earth in jets and rockets. One day he hit upon the idea of using sunlight pressure to move vehicles through space. In 1924 he proposed building a one-ton craft with a mirrored surface measuring approximately 19 million square yards (16 million square meters).

About the same time, Fridrikh Tsander (1886?–1933), a Russian engineer, also realized the advantages of using sunlight for space travel. He imagined using huge sheets of thin mirrors to reflect photons, and he envisioned a time when mammoth space vehicles could be built on stations in **orbit** around the Earth.

The National Aeronautics and Space Administration (NASA), the United States government agency that oversees space exploration, also became aware of photon pressure early in its space program. In 1958 NASA scientists placed small metal needles in orbit above the Earth as part of a communications study. When the needles were eventually pushed out of their orbit, scientists concluded that sunlight pressure had provided the push.

NASA was also able to use photon pressure to solve a problem during one of its space probe missions. In 1974 *Mariner 10* passed Venus and was heading for Mercury, when a problem developed

The National Aeronautics and Space Administration first used photon pressure to correct a problem encountered by Mariner 10 *as it passed Venus* (above) *on its way to Mars.*

in the spacecraft's control system. The spacecraft was heading off course. Using the craft's rockets to correct the problem would have used up too much fuel. Engineers on the ground decided instead to turn the craft's two solar panels to receive a push from the Sun. The maneuver was successful, and *Mariner 10* was able to complete its Mercury flyby.

An artist's sketch shows a fully deployed space sail.

Support for Sails Grows

The ideas of Tsiolkovsky and Tsander, which had mostly been looked upon with skepticism, resurfaced in an article by Carl Wiley entitled "Clipper Ships of Space." It appeared in the May 1951 issue of the magazine *Astounding Science Fiction*. Wiley, an aeronautical engineer, described how sails would someday be used for space travel. The article inspired a number of scientists to examine space sailing more closely. As they did, their enthusiasm grew.

In 1958 another article on the subject appeared, this time in the magazine *Jet Propulsion*. Its author was Richard Garwin, a physicist at IBM and Columbia University. Garwin believed sailing could one day become a practical way of traveling through space.

That same year, Ted Cotter of the Los Alamos Scientific Laboratory described a plan for using sails that spin. Just as sails on seagoing ships must be kept taut for maximum efficiency, so must space sails. While masts and ropes or chains are used on boats to keep sails rigid, Cotter's spinning sails would use **centrifugal force** (a force that pushes an object outward from its center of rotation).

In 1967 Richard MacNeal of Astro Research Corporation presented NASA with a plan for a type of sail called a heliogyro. Its long narrow blades, made of a thin and highly reflective material, resembled helicopter rotors. MacNeal and his partner, John Hedgepath, suggested using this spacecraft for pilotless missions to planets near the Earth. Larger models could be built to carry astronauts.

NASA, however, was unable to work on any sail projects because of cutbacks in government funding for space exploration. It was not until the 1970s that scientists at the space agency began looking again at light pressure as a means of propelling spacecraft.

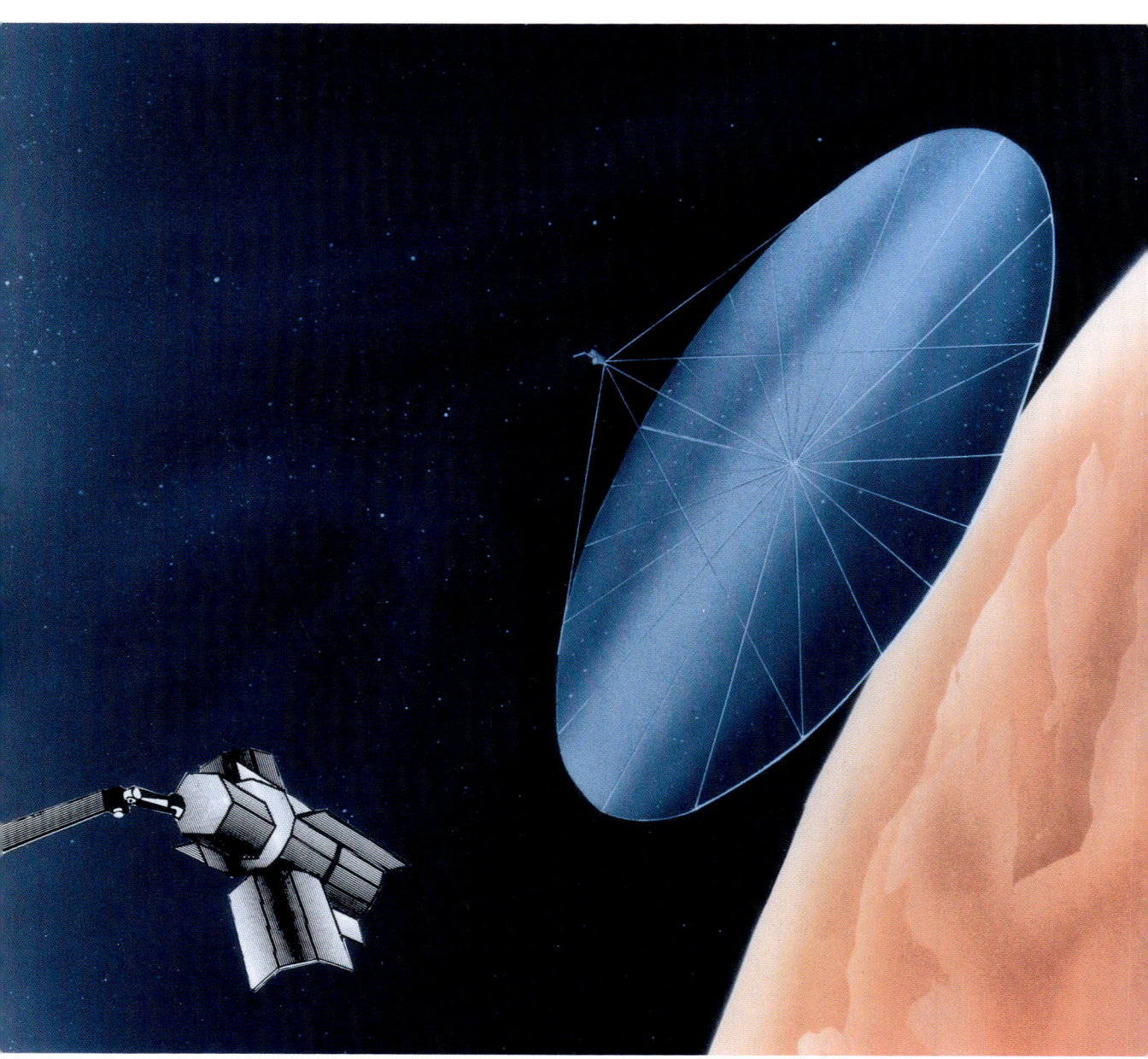

A disk sail is one of the many designs being considered.

2

Designing and Building a Sail

Imagine a giant sail made of highly reflective material. In space, well beyond the pull of the Earth's gravity, photons hit the sail and cause it to move. The forward motion is quite slow at first, perhaps only about three feet (one meter) in an hour. But the sail will be moving as fast as 2,200 miles (3,540 km) per hour in just a few months, and the craft will still be accelerating.

Although faster at first, a rocket-powered spacecraft will eventually run out of fuel and be forced to coast. A sail, however, will require no fuel. The push will be constant as long as the Sun shines on the sail, and the speed of the sail will continue to increase year after year.

Scientists realized a space sail would have to be made of a material that reflects as many photons as possible. It would also have to be extremely large, perhaps extending over as much as several miles. The larger the sail, the greater the number of photons that will hit it.

Choosing the Material

Scientists experimented with many different materials but found none to be a perfect reflector. Some photons, instead of bouncing off, were absorbed by the materials they tested.

Silver, although a good reflector, eventually loses its luster. Aluminum works well, but it wrinkles easily, which could cause "hot spots" in the sail. The

Many scientists believe Kapton—shown here in the manufacturing process—to be the best material for constructing space sails.

effect would be the same as focusing the rays of the Sun through a magnifying glass onto a dry leaf, which can cause it to catch fire.

Aluminum would need to be kept smooth while folded and carried into space. Spraying sheets of plastic with a thin layer of aluminum could help solve the wrinkling problem. The plastic, however, must be light if the sail is to move as effortlessly as possible through space. Ordinary plastic wrap is about .0005 inches (.0128 millimeters) thick. Plastic even this thin is too thick for sails.

After conducting experiments with more than 25 different materials, scientists found Kapton, a plastic material manufactured by the Du Pont chemical company, to be the most satisfactory. Tissuelike sheets of Kapton, many times thinner than a human hair, were found to be durable enough to withstand the rigors of space flight. A square Kapton sail, measuring approximately 100 feet (30 m) on each side, would weigh only about 220 pounds (100 kg). It would be resistant to the damaging effects of sunlight, easy to manufacture, and durable.

Protecting the Sail

Next, the sail would have to be protected from a variety of dangers it might encounter in space. Meteoroids and other rocky particles left over from the formation of the Solar System (the Sun and the planets that travel around it) whirl through space. These particles could puncture a sail without causing too much damage, but they must not be allowed to rip it.

The sails of a boat are strengthened by thick seams called ripstops, which keep the wind from tearing them. Similarly, a Kapton sail would have to be either doubled in various places or reinforced with tape to prevent ripping.

Also, a sail could be severely damaged if it encounters the electrically charged particles in solar winds. The high voltages contained in these winds could disrupt radio communications with the Earth and might even destroy sensitive electronic guidance and control instruments on board the craft. Metal grounding straps would have to be installed on the sail to direct the flow of dangerous electrical currents away from the equipment.

A space sail flying through very high temperatures could also easily overheat and cause the sail material to sag. A special coating on the sail could prevent this problem by reflecting the heat into space.

In addition, the sail would have to be kept from fluttering as it maneuvers in space. As described earlier, one way to keep the sail rigid would be to make it spin. Another method would be to at-

The disk sail (above) *and the heliogyro sail* (facing page) *show the variety of designs scientists are working on.*

tach the space sail to supports similar to those used with sails on boats.

Designing the Sail

The simplest sail design being considered is the disk, which consists of a large circular sheet of reflective material. Since the disk would spin around a central axis, no supporting structure would be required.

Another design is the heliogyro, the idea of Richard MacNeal and John Hedgepath. It would have from 2 to 12 long Kapton blades attached to a hub and edged with a lightweight tape to help prevent ripping. Plastic supports could also be placed in various spots along each blade for extra strength.

A third design is the kitelike sail—that could be square, rectangular, triangular, or any other shape—which would be attached to supports to prevent flapping.

How large should the sail be? Scientists knew that sails of any size would accelerate, but a small sail would be struck by fewer photons than a large one and would travel more slowly. The larger the sail, the faster it would move.

Scientists also had to consider the sail's cargo, since the amount of cargo would also affect the sail's speed. To compensate for the burden of necessary equipment, the size of the sail would have to be increased. It might be nec-

essary for a square sail, for example, to be hundreds of feet long on each side, or for a heliogyro to have blades several miles long!

Mass and Density

When scientists want to know how heavy something is, they use the term **mass**, which is the amount of matter something contains. An object's mass and weight might be the same on Earth, but the same object will weigh less in space because of the decrease in gravity. Its mass, however, will remain unchanged—it still contains the same amount of matter.

Density indicates how loosely, or how tightly, mass is packed together. A one-pound piece of cloth has less density than a one-pound rock because the cloth's mass is spread out over a larger area than that of the rock.

The lower a sail's density, the faster it will accelerate in space. A sail with a mass of 1 ounce (28 grams) spread over approximately 10 square feet (1 sq m) of material will accelerate faster than one with a mass of 10 ounces (280 g) spread over the same area.

Construction

How could the mammoth sails possibly be built on Earth?

In the case of the heliogyro, the sail material might first be manufactured in rolls similar to giant packages of aluminum foil or plastic wrap. The material could be gradually unrolled, taped, coated, and reinforced with plastic supports, ripstops, and whatever else might be needed. Each section could be rerolled onto larger reels as it was completed. The reels could then be attached to each other to form the heliogyro.

To construct the disk and kite sails, several rolls of material would be unrolled, positioned side by side, and taped together to form a section. After a section was completed, it could then be folded or rolled into a smaller unit. The process would be slow and tedious, but scientists were convinced it could be done.

To help work out design problems, engineers built a model of a sail making machine.

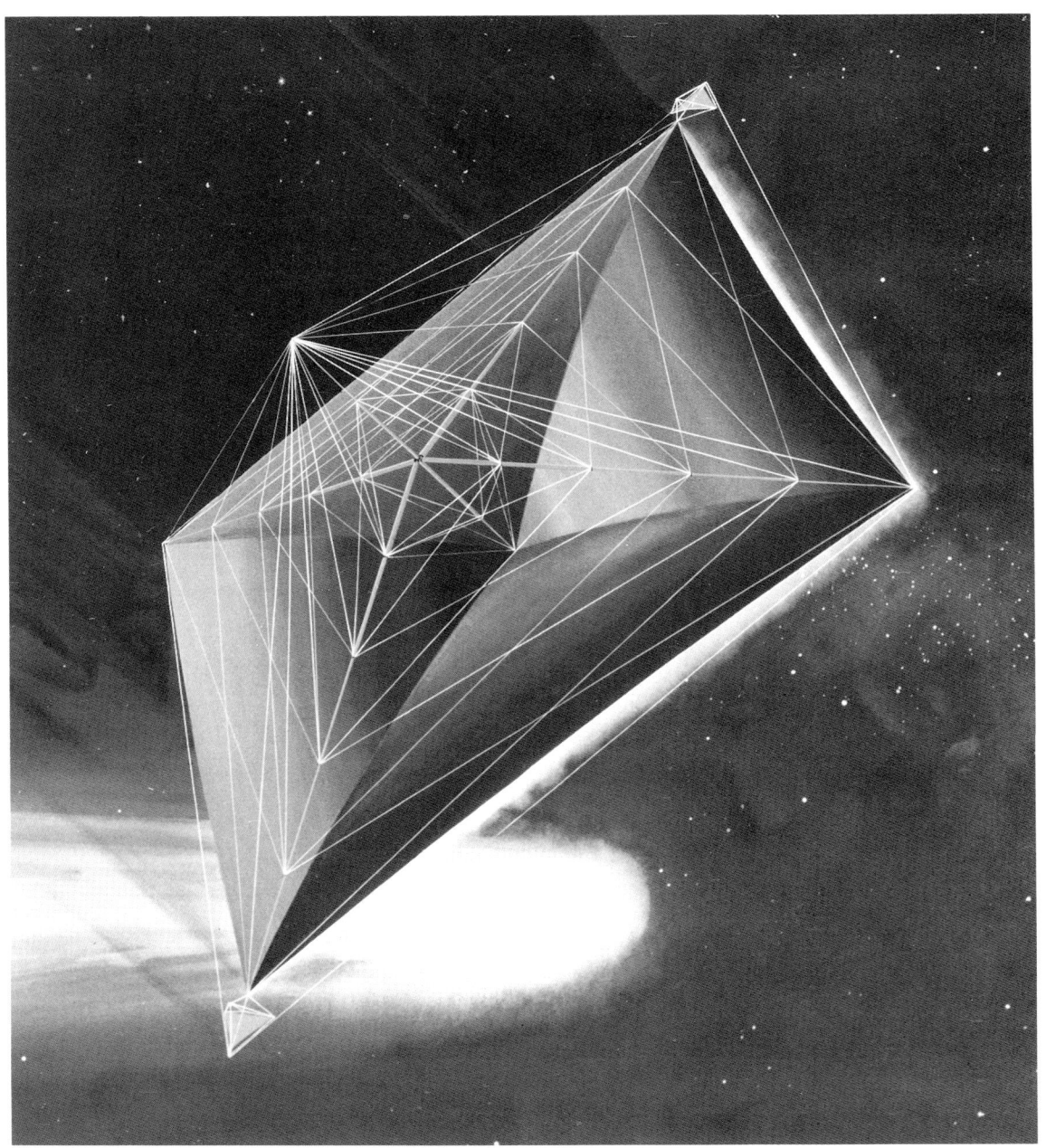

Artists pictured two types of sails nearing Halley's comet, the square sail (facing page) *and the heliogyro sail* (above).

Packaging and Launching

Packaging and transporting sails into space would be a major problem. The heliogyro blades would have to be rolled up and then wired together around a central hub. Once in space, the blades would unroll as the craft began spinning. It might take several hours for the sail to completely unfurl. The ease with which the heliogyro could be launched was one of the main reasons many scientists favored its design.

Packing the kite sail—in particular, the square sail—would not be too difficult. Launching it in space, however, might be more complicated than launching either the heliogyro or the disk. First supports, called **spars**, would have to unroll from around the central drum or cargo unit. From a ribbonlike shape, they would slowly form long tubes similar to the structures used on the soil-sampling arms of the Viking Mars landers. Wires at the ends of the spars would pull each of the sail's four corners, opening the sail and attaching it to the ends of the spars. Because it is a complex procedure during which several things could go wrong, scientists thought robots, or even astronauts, might have to monitor the launching.

Reaching Escape Velocity

Earth's gravity pulls all things downward, regardless of their weight. When you throw an object into the air, it falls to the ground after reaching a certain height. If you could throw the object at a speed of about 24,800 miles (40,000 km) per hour, however, it would not fall back to Earth. This speed is known as the Earth's **escape velocity**.

Since sails cannot reach escape velocity by themselves in the Earth's atmosphere, they would have to be carried into space by a rocket. Folded or rolled and placed in the nose of a rocket, or in the cargo bay of a **space shuttle**, sails could be transported beyond Earth's gravity for launching.

Steering the Sail

Scientists also had to determine how to steer a sail and control its speed. A sail cannot be steered in the same way an airplane is steered. An airplane turns when air pushes against flaps on its wings and tail. But there is no air in space for a spacecraft to push against. Most conventional spaceships utilize small rockets placed in various positions aboard the craft to maintain the desired course. The thrust created by firing these rockets moves the ship in the desired direction. How could sails be made to move in different directions?

Sailors can change the direction of their ship at sea by adjusting its sails in relationship to the wind. Space sails could be constructed to maneuver in a similar way. If a sail is angled away from the Sun, fewer photons will strike it, the ship's speed will decrease, and it will be drawn by the Sun's gravity and drift closer to its surface. If a sail is angled toward the sunlight, more photons will bombard it, the craft's speed will increase, and it will move away from the Sun.

On a disk sail, one solution for steering would be to place a system of tracks and lines at the center of the craft. By hanging the cargo from these lines and shifting it from side to side along the tracks, the sail could be steered.

The blades of a heliogyro could be tilted in relationship to the Sun, thereby changing the ship's direction. In the kite sail, the main sail and smaller sails could be tilted. Power for these maneuvers on each type of sail could be provided by solar cells and batteries stored on board the craft.

This heliogyro sail has spokes stretching out over 3.7 miles (6 km) and can carry instruments on board a spacecraft.

Many scientists from around the world are designing space sails to travel toward Halley's comet.

3

International Competition

In 1973 NASA hired Jerome Wright of the Battelle Memorial Institute in Ohio to examine various sail designs and possible methods of using sails to reach other planets. In the course of his work, Wright proposed using space sails to undergo a **rendezvous**—or planned meeting—with Halley's comet.

The comet travels in 76-year-long orbits, and it was expected to reappear in the inner Solar System in 1986. Scientists around the world were already designing and building spaceships to enable them to observe the comet at close range. But the idea of an actual rendezvous was unique. A spaceship would not merely fly past the comet but would actually travel with it.

While the Earth and the other planets orbit the Sun in one direction, Halley's comet traces an opposite path. To accomplish a rendezvous, an orbiting spacecraft would have to first come to a stop, then gain enough speed in the opposite direction to keep up with the comet.

When a group of scientists at the Jet Propulsion Laboratory (JPL) heard of Wright's proposal, they invited him to their headquarters in California to explain the procedure. Wright described how a solar sail could be used to move a craft close to the Sun and gain enough altitude to move over the top of it. The sail would then be traveling in a clockwise orbit. Within four years, it would

An artist has shown the European Space Agency's spacecraft, Giotto, *nearing Halley's comet.*

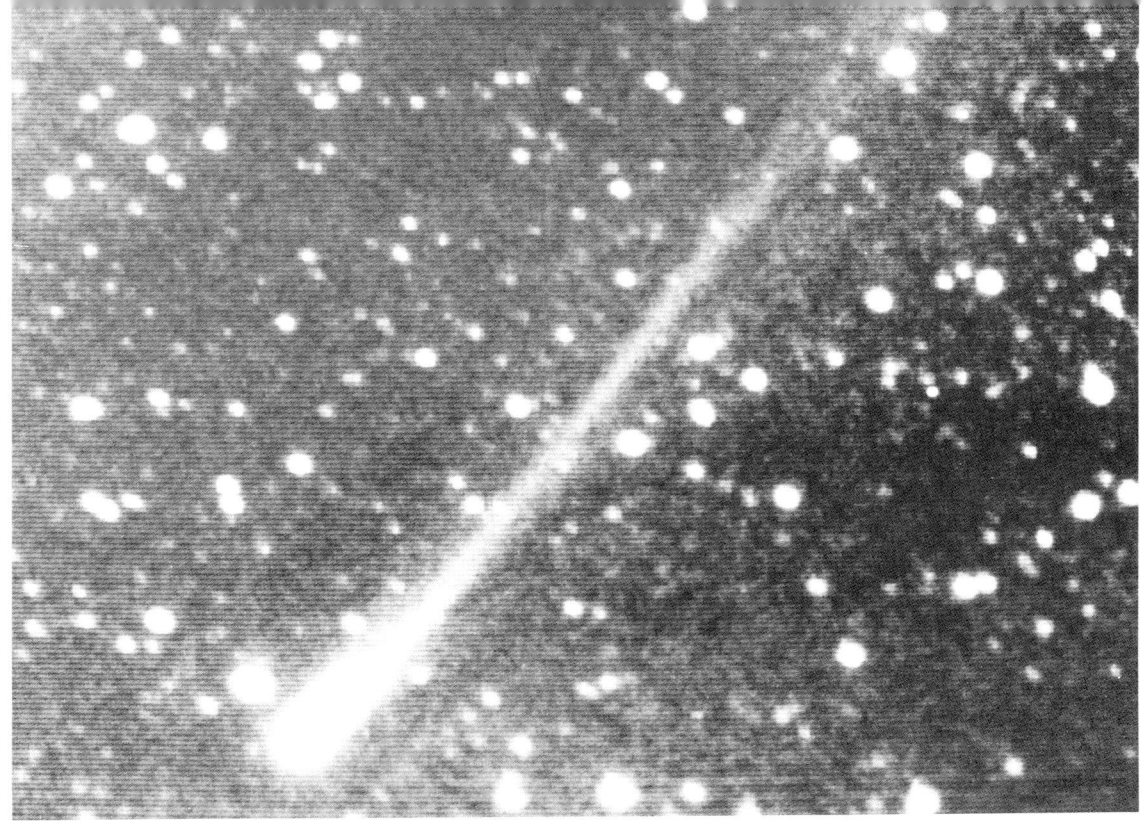

Halley's comet, which travels in 76-year orbits, is shown here in a 1910 photograph as it neared the Earth.

reach the speed of the comet—about 25 miles (40 km) per second or close to 90,000 miles (145,000 km) per hour —as the comet entered the inner Solar System.

The JPL group persuaded Wright to join them on a Halley's comet project. In 1975, with funding from NASA, the team of scientists began working against time in order to meet the comet's scheduled arrival. The spaceship had to be built and launched by 1981. NASA's Ames and Langley research centers and several industrial contractors, such as Hughes Aircraft and McDonnell Douglas, offered to help with the project.

NASA was working on a space shuttle at the same time. The comet project team hoped to package their sail and place it on board the shuttle for launch into an Earth orbit. From there the sail would begin the maneuvers that would lead it to a rendezvous with Halley's comet.

After a year of working on the proposals, the JPL team decided that a 12-blade heliogyro would be the most suitable craft for the Halley's comet mission. NASA began having doubts about the project, however, since its shuttle program was behind schedule and congressional funding was becoming scarce. The agency also feared the sail project was too risky and insufficiently tested for such a rigorous trip. In 1977, before the sail could be built, NASA withdrew its support.

By the time Halley's comet appeared in 1986, five spacecraft had been launched to study it: the Soviet Union's *Vega 1* and *Vega 2*, Japan's *Suisei* and *Sakigake,* and the European Space Agency's *Giotto.* Unfortunately, no space sail was among them.

World Space Foundation

Despite this setback, the idea of solar sailing continued to capture the imagination of space enthusiasts around the world. In 1979 Wright and a group of fellow scientists, many of whom were

The stars appeared blurred in this time lapse photograph taken in 1986 as Halley's comet again approached the Earth.

from JPL, decided to set up a private, nonprofit organization to continue work on the sail. The organization was named the World Space Foundation (WSF), and headquarters were established in Pasadena, California. Members chose not to depend on government funding. Instead, they asked private businesses and individuals to support and participate in various space projects.

One of the goals of the group was to place a small sail in space. Once it was demonstrated that a sail could be successfully launched and maneuvered, other sails could be built. Some might explore various asteroids and others could be used to transport equipment to various planets. An entire fleet of sails could carry supplies to Mars in advance of a landing expedition, and—one day— sails might even participate in a journey to the stars.

Model Sail Tested

Space engineers donated their spare time, corporations gave advice and equipment, and individuals and groups offered financial support to the organization. On August 25, 1981, WSF participated in an exhibition called Planetfest at the Pasadena Civic Center to celebrate *Voyager 2*—a remote-controlled space probe—and its encounter with Saturn. While speakers, displays, and demonstrations on a variety of topics

were featured, the highlight of the event was the ground testing of a model solar sail by WSF members.

The square-shaped sail was made of Mylar (plastic similar to Kapton) and measured 46 feet (14 m) on each side. It was about one-fourth the size of the actual sail they hoped to eventually launch in space.

Volunteers assembled the sail by unrolling strips of Mylar on a long table. The edge of each strip was taped to the next one and then folded on top of it. The strips were wrapped around a drumlike structure representing the spacecraft's cargo bay. Two pairs of thin stainless steel tubes, were attached to the sail.

At test time, one pair of spars automatically began unrolling from the drum, and with it unrolled the wrapped sail. Wires at the ends of the second pair of spars pulled open the accordionfolded sail to form a flat sheet. Everything went as planned, and the scientists knew they were one step closer to actually launching a sail.

A Race to the Moon and Beyond

A number of engineers from the French National Space Agency were also conducting a study of solar sails at about the same time. They called themselves the Union Pour la Promotion de la Propulsion Photonique (U3P). In 1981,

Between the design stage and actual construction of the space sails, scientists built mock-ups of the spacecraft.

to stimulate interest in their project, the U3P scientists proposed a solar sailing race to the Moon. They managed to persuade a regional government in France to sponsor the race and offer prizes.

Intrigued by the plan, the American Institute of Aeronautics and Astronautics (AIAA) began encouraging various groups in the United States to design and compete in the race.

Congress created the Columbus Quincentenary Jubilee Commission in 1984 to plan and organize activities in the United States for the celebration of the 500th anniversary of Columbus's voyage to America. Commission members saw the sail race as a way to commemorate Columbus's voyage as well as to stimulate space study and exploration. Some scientists hoped the spacecraft would sail not only to the Moon but also to Mars.

Entries from countries around the world were welcomed, but no direct government funding was allowed. The spacecraft could be any size or shape but could not use any means of propulsion other than pressure from sunlight.

Designs from around the World

Imaginative individuals worked at their drawing boards and computers for the next few years, designing sails for the competition. In November 1989, a committee appointed by the AIAA selected eight finalists: three from the United States; one from a joint effort by France and Spain; and one each from Japan, the Soviet Union, Canada, and England.

The sails included a variety of designs and sizes. The English sail was disk-shaped with flexible plastic ribbing running through it. The disk would cover about 15 acres (6.07 hectares). It was expected to reach Mars in less than one year, making it one of the fastest sails entered in the race.

The French/Spanish design had four masts, each 148 feet (45 m) long. The sail itself would be of either Kapton or a similar material, aluminized on both sides. The total area would be slightly larger than five baseball diamonds.

Japan's entry called for a sail 330 feet (100 m) on each side. It was eventually scaled down, however, to 98 feet (30 m) on a side. Canadian scientists proposed a hexagonal design of 12,000 square yards (10,000 sq m).

A team of graduate students at the Massachusetts Institute of Technology designed one of the three U.S. selections. It was a heliogyro with eight rotors, each 275 feet (84 m) long and 5 feet (1.5 m) wide. These would be made of Kapton or Lexan, a lightweight film used in model aircraft construction. When completed, the blades would be rolled up and stored in the upper part of a Pegasus rocket, a U.S. launch vehicle. After release, the craft would begin

In 1993 Russia became the first country to actually launch a solar sail. An experimental reflector called Znamya was assembled by cosmonauts (Russian astronauts) aboard the Mir space station. They then placed the folded sail in Earth orbit, where it mechanically unfolded to form a disk. Tests were then conducted to determine how the sail could be maneuvered in space.

spinning at about one rotation per minute, as the blades gradually unrolled. The process of unfolding the sail was expected to take about 30 minutes.

A group of scientists at Johns Hopkins University in Maryland submitted another of the U.S. designs. In the shape of a sunflower, it had 480 petal-shaped sails held flat by a large hoop. When constructed, the entire craft would measure about 560 feet (170 m) in diameter. Each of the petals would be individually rolled and carried into space aboard a Pegasus rocket. Once in orbit, the sails would begin unrolling, taking approximately 20 minutes to fully open.

The third U.S. design was submitted by the WSF scientists. They had a seven-year head start, having worked on a number of designs dating back to the Halley's comet project at JPL. They chose a square Kapton sail, 180 feet (55 m) on each side. At each of the sail's corners were smaller triangular sails to help control the craft. Before being launched into space, the sail would be folded into a small package and secured around a hub so that it could later be drawn away and unfolded. The unfurling would take an estimated 48 minutes.

Participants had to overcome numerous problems. Many assumed the Jubilee Commission would help raise money to build the spacecraft, which were expected to cost from $3 million to $15 million each. When fund-raising became impossible for the Commission, individual teams were forced to either find their own sponsors or withdraw.

The field eventually narrowed to three sails. The French/Spanish sail would represent Europe, from which Columbus had begun his journey, and the Japanese sail would represent Asia, where he had hoped to arrive. The WSF sail proposal, determined by AIAA committee members to be the "best managed" and "most technically grounded" of the U.S. entries, would represent the Americas, where Columbus actually landed.

To reach their goal, the WSF scientists working on the U.S. entry needed help. Groups such as the Charles A. Lindbergh Foundation, Hughes Aircraft, United Technologies, and the California Space Institute contributed thousands of dollars in funds and equipment.

Technical assistance was offered by scientists at JPL, McDonnell Douglas, Aura Systems Inc., the Amateur Radio Satellite Corporation, Utah State University, Weber College, and the Planetary Society. Emerson LaBombard, previously at McDonnell Douglas, became the director of the project.

Sail designers soon realized they needed more time to obtain financial support and to construct their sails. In

1991 leaders of the WSF, the U3P of Europe, and the Solar Sail Union of Japan met and formed an Earth-Moon Race Committee. The committee established rules for the race and made plans to publicize the event, known as the Luna Cup Race, which is scheduled for 1995.

In August of 1991, the Earth-Moon Race Committee announced that the European Space Agency's *Ariane 4* rocket would be used as a launch vehicle, and that only the WSF sail would continue the journey to Mars. Because of its advanced design, the WSF spacecraft—called the *Solar Sail Race Vehicle (SSRV)*—would also be responsible for a number of pre-race tasks.

The *SSRV* would support the other sails during launch, and then its communication system would be responsible for tracking all the sails. The Japanese sail would be carried inside the French/Spanish sail, and the *SSRV* would be positioned beneath them. After separation from the launch vehicle, the Japanese and French/Spanish sails would travel together on the *SSRV*. They would all begin spinning together at about 65 to 90 revolutions per minute. A small rocket aboard the *SSRV* would then fire, raising the three craft to a higher orbit.

The sails would gradually stop spinning, and the three craft would separate

July 1985: The European Space Agency's Ariane 4 *blasts off.*

from each other. For the next two to three weeks, the sails would remain behind an imaginary starting line, while ground crews took them through various maneuvers.

Because the WSF sail would be carrying more equipment than the others, certain allowances would be made so that each entry would have an equal chance of winning.

36

The Flight Plan

At the start of the race, the sails would begin traveling toward the Moon, a journey that would take from six months to one year. The first sail to send back pictures of the far side of the Moon would be declared the winner. Prizes would be awarded for the first to finish, for the sail making the most efficient use of photons, and for the best-piloted craft.

The SSRV would then become a research vehicle and continue its journey to Mars. WSF scientists hoped to take advantage of the so-called "Mars window." Approximately every 26 months, Earth and Mars line up, making possible the shortest and most direct trip between the two planets. If this "window" were missed, the trip to Mars might take longer than the estimated two and one-half years.

During the second lap of the mission, various scientific experiments involving cosmic dust, magnetic fields, and communications would be conducted.

Also on board the SSRV would be a time capsule containing digital reproductions of essays, poems, songs, and pictures expressing the thoughts, hopes, and dreams of millions of young people around the world. After passing Mars, the sail might continue its journey through space for many more years. The scientists hope that someday, a space traveler from another planet will find and decode the messages from Earth.

In early 1993, Russia launched a solar sail aboard a *Progress M-15* automated cargo spacecraft. After *Progress* docked with the *Mir* space station, two cosmonauts (Russian astronauts) assembled the sail. The spacecraft then backed about 500 feet (150 meters) away from the space station and released the sail. The sail began to unfold, forming a disk that measured 65 feet (20 m) in diameter. Not only did it move, but the sail also reflected sunlight that was visible in various places on Earth.

When the Luna Cup Race is held, scientists from other countries hope the Russians, making use of whatever discoveries they have made about space sailing, will also take part in the event.

As they travel through space, sails will encounter gravitational forces from other planets they encounter such as Saturn shown here.

4

In Space

Once a solar sail is released from its orbiting launch vehicle, it must escape the pull of Earth's gravity and the drag, or slowdown, caused by friction with its atmosphere. In a low Earth orbit, the pull of gravity and the friction of air particles can cause spacecraft to lose altitude.

Skylab, America's first space station, was launched in 1973. Atmospheric drag pulled it out of orbit six years later, and it burned up as it reentered the Earth's atmosphere. Remnants of the craft were scattered over the Indian Ocean and parts of Australia.

A solar sail can overcome this pull by angling itself to receive the maximum amount of sunlight each time it orbits

Earth. It can eventually pick up enough speed to escape atmospheric drag, but this is a time-consuming maneuver. Another method would be to use a booster rocket to raise the vehicle to a higher orbit.

Space sails will not always be able to move forward in straight lines. To avoid the shifting crosscurrents of gravitational forces from the Earth, Moon, Sun, and other planets they might encounter in their travels, the sails will have to take looping paths, or **trajectories**.

Gravity Assists

A sail approaching the Moon might take any of three trajectories. One, it might simply fly past the Moon; two,

NASA's Mariner 10 spacecraft was the first to use gravity assists in its journey from Venus to Mercury.

the sail could approach close enough to be captured by the Moon's gravity and then move into an orbit around the Moon; or three, the sail could allow itself to be thrown by the force of the Moon's gravity into a higher trajectory by a process called a **gravity assist**.

In a gravity assist, a sail would keep accelerating as it approached the Moon. Because the Moon would be traveling faster than the sail, the Moon's gravitational field would literally pull the sail along with it, increasing the craft's speed at the same time. When the sail got to the other side of the Moon, it would shoot off into space like a pebble shot from a slingshot.

Mariner 10 first made use of a gravity assist when it flew from Venus to Mercury. *Voyager 1* moved from Jupiter to Saturn this way, and *Voyager 2* went to Uranus in 1986 and to Neptune in 1989 by making use of this same technique.

Communications, Power, and Control

As they do with other spacecraft, powerful ground-based tracking systems must monitor space sails at all times. Signals will be sent to the craft, and

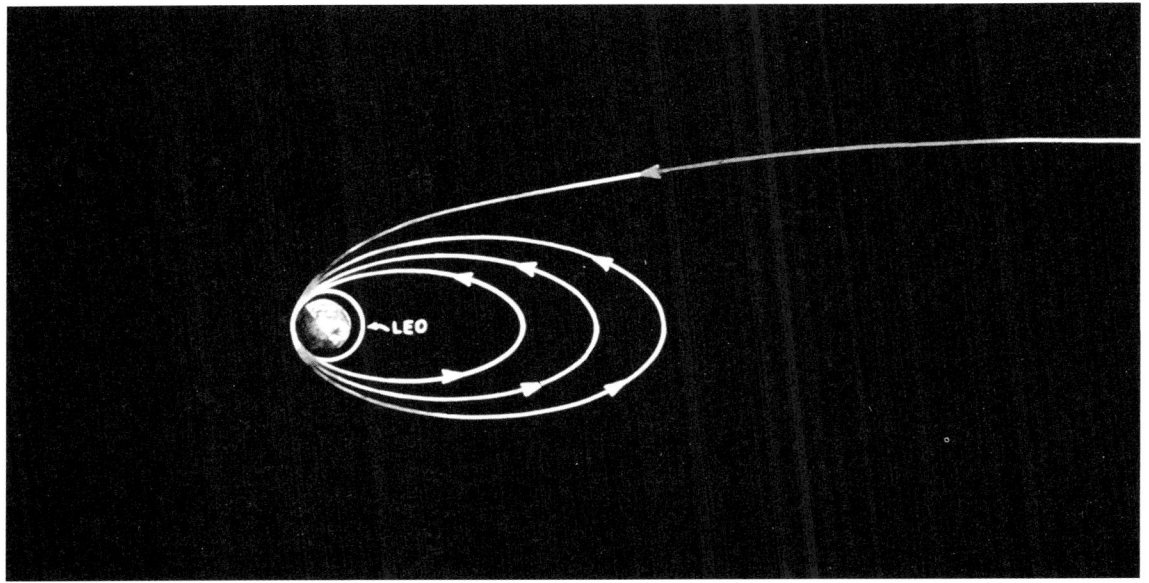

Depending upon the angle of approach, a sail might be pulled into an orbit around the Moon (shown here), or it could be thrown into a higher trajectory in a gravity assist.

A square solar sail proposed by NASA-Jet Propulsion Laboratory scientists could be used to receive freight packages carried to it by the space shuttle for delivery to the Moon, Mars, or asteroids.

different sails will receive the signals in different ways. Some craft will have sensors—which receive the signals—scattered over their sails, while others will carry sensors along with scientific equipment in their cargo bays.

The *SSRV* cargo bay, which is at the center of the craft, is designed to hold position sensors, data processing for the ship's autopilot, solar panels, antennae, and a television camera on a boom that can extend to 9 feet (2.7 m). The camera is capable of turning in various directions and of relaying to Earth images of the Moon, asteroids, and planets. It will also send back pictures of the sail so that ground crews can continually monitor its condition and performance.

To monitor changes in a space sail's direction of travel, high-powered sensors will focus on several reference points, such as the Sun and the Earth. If the craft angles away from the intended direction of travel, the sensors will detect the change and a computer on board will activate the systems needed to bring the sail back on course. For example, the blades of a heliogyro will be turned toward or away from the Sun, or smaller sails on the ends of a square sail will be turned slightly, helping to stabilize the ship.

Solar panels on the craft will collect power from the Sun and store it in batteries for backup power.

Importance of Radar

A journey to the Moon or Mars will require scientists to know at all times where the sail is in the vastness of space, how fast it is going, and how far it is from its destination. **Radar**, or strong pulses of radio waves, will be an important means of making these measurements.

Traveling at the speed of light, radar waves sent from control centers on Earth will bounce off sails in space and return. Scientists monitoring these signals will be able to pinpoint not only the position of the sail but also its distance from various bodies in the Solar System. Radar will also help determine the sail's velocity (its speed in a particular direction).

This ground station, in communication with three satellites, replaced NASA's entire worldwide tracking network.

Aiming for Moving Targets

Journeys to other planets will involve traveling millions of miles. The Moon, the closest body to Earth, is only 240,000 miles (386,000 km) away. Venus is 26 million miles (42 million km) from the Earth, and Jupiter is 390 million miles (628 million km) away, both at the closest points in their orbit around the Sun. Trips to these planets can take months and years, depending upon the speed of the craft.

Seafarers of long ago sailed toward distant continents that were stationary. Space sails, however, will head for targets that are constantly moving. Not only do the planets rotate on their **axes**, they also move around the Sun at different rates of speed. The Earth, traveling at 67,000 miles (107,800 km) per hour, takes one year to revolve around the Sun. Mars, moving more slowly, takes 687 days, and Jupiter takes 11.86 years.

Planets follow slightly oval, or elliptical, paths rather than circular ones. At certain times, they come closer to the Earth than at other times. Mars, for example, is about 35 million miles (56 million km) away at its closest point to the Earth. If a sail waited until Mars reached this position before heading toward it, the planet would be long gone by the time the craft arrived at that spot. To reach any target in the Solar System requires advance planning and precise calculations that must be continually updated.

In addition to solar winds and meteorites discussed earlier, there are other hazards. Sails must avoid being caught in the gravitational fields of planets and dragged into the atmospheres that exist on some of them. Also, sails headed beyond Mars face the threat of thousands of irregularly shaped rocks orbiting in the asteroid belts.

Why would scientists choose sails instead of less fragile spaceships? One clear advantage is that sails do not require bulky and expensive fuels. They are also less likely to have a negative impact on the space environment. The full effect on the Earth's atmosphere and on the space environment of huge amounts of spent chemicals from rockets is unknown. Sails offer a safer alternative.

Humans may colonize Mars within the next century, but before colonization can take place, hundreds of tons of equipment and supplies will have to be brought to the planet.

A U.S. shuttle, on a single trip, could carry only about 5 tons (4.5 metric tons) of cargo to Mars and then would require refueling before it could return to Earth. By contrast, a square sail measuring just .5 mile (805 m) on each side could deliver close to 6.5 tons (5.9 t) to Mars. Without a need for refueling, it could then return to Earth orbit, pick up more cargo, and sail off again.

Sails could eventually travel toward planets as close as Mercury and Venus, and as far away as Jupiter and Saturn. They could also be used to help explore asteroids.

Since sails are capable of traveling at high speeds, they will be able to move out of elliptical orbits more easily than other spacecraft. *Ulysses*, the satellite the European Space Agency launched in 1990 to observe the poles on the Sun, first has to travel to Jupiter. There it will receive a gravity assist and be flung into the desired orbit around the Sun in 1994 and 1995. A solar craft, by comparison, would need only to tilt its sails and receive an extra push from photons to change orbit.

A disk sail is shown maneuvering through outer space.

Scientists are already at work designing space sails that could travel to distant galaxies.

5

To the Stars

Space travel will continue to change dramatically in the future. For example, the construction of the NASA space station *Freedom*, scheduled to begin in 1995, will make possible new methods of building and launching vehicles.

Scientist Eric Drexler, author of the book *Engines of Creation*, has envisioned constructing huge sails in space. His plans call for sails made of carbon-fiber strings in a meshlike pattern. The gaps between the strings would be as large as football fields and would be covered with panels of extremely thin aluminum foil. The sails would be kept rigid by centrifugal force.

British-American physicist Freeman Dyson has designed another version. His mesh sails would use highly reflective strings without the aluminum foil between them. The sails would be larger and lighter than Drexler's, and their speed even faster. Since they would catch less air, they could move closer to a planet's atmosphere without the risk of being pulled out of their orbit.

To avoid the atmospheric drag that might affect sail construction on board a space station, John Garvey of McDonnell Douglas has suggested building a platform on the station and then releasing it to a higher orbit. It could contain scaffolding, a power-generating system, a crane for hoisting the sail, and a pressurized cabin for the workers. Such a system could produce an entire fleet of

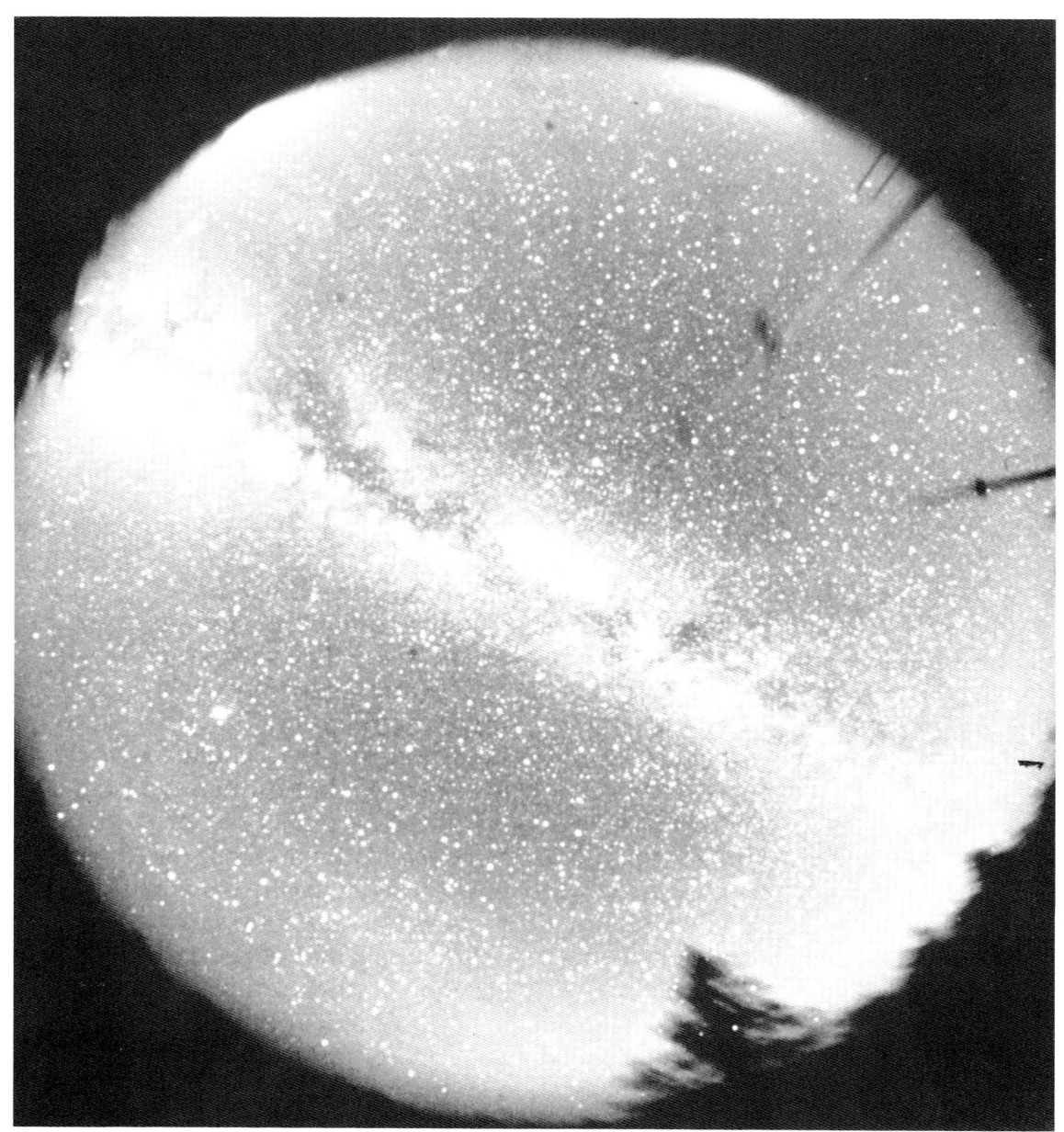

A wide-angle view of the Milky Way from the Earth

sails that might travel not only to the planets but to the stars.

As vast as our Solar System is, it is only a pinpoint in the entire universe. The Milky Way galaxy, of which the Earth is a part, consists of more than two hundred billion stars and huge swirling clouds of gas and dust, where new stars are constantly taking shape. The entire mass spins slowly. Our Solar System takes about 200 million years just to make one revolution. Beyond the Milky Way are billions of other galaxies with other stars spinning inside them.

The size of the universe is unknown. When distances in the universe are calculated, **light-years** are used as units of measurement. A light-year is the distance that light, racing at 186,300 miles (299,800 km) per second, travels in one year. A light-year is almost 6 trillion miles (9.7 trillion km).

The Milky Way is 100,000 light-years in diameter. Light from the Alpha Centauri system, the star system nearest to the Sun, travels for 4.3 years to reach the Earth.

Voyager 2, which is heading away from our Solar System at 30,000 miles (48,280 km) per hour, will take more than 94,000 years just to reach the Alpha Centauri system. For human interstellar travel to ever become possible, faster spacecraft will have to be designed.

Light from the Orion nebula travels for 1,500 years before reaching the Earth.

49

Alternative Power Sources

Many other ideas for powering interstellar vehicles have been proposed. Project Daedalus, a study by the British Interplanetary Society, uses a nuclear pulse rocket powered by hundreds of thousands of hydrogen bombs. Exploding approximately one each second from a spacecraft would give tremendous momentum to the ship.

Another proposal calls for the use of intense energy particles. Scientists have discovered that when particles called **antimatter** come into contact with the regular atomic particles of ordinary matter under certain conditions, both are destroyed. Intense energy is created in the process. Scientists theorize that if enough of these opposing particles were used, the energy generated could accelerate a craft to nearly the speed of light.

Before the spacecraft for any of these proposals can be built, however, many technical problems must be solved, and the cost will undoubtedly be high.

Only solar-powered sails now appear capable of attaining the desired speed without the huge expense. Before sails head for the stars, however, another problem must be overcome. The push from photons becomes weaker the farther the sail moves from the Sun. Even with gravity assists from distant planets, sails would take more than 6,000 years to reach the Alpha Centauri system. One solution may be the use of artificial light.

Development of Lasers

Ordinary artificial light, such as that from a flashlight, consists of waves that vibrate in many different directions. The farther the light waves travel, the more they spread out. By contrast, light from a **laser** consists of highly concentrated light waves that are capable of traveling great distances without spreading.

The first laser was built in 1960 by Theodore Maiman. He used a rod of synthetic ruby, a man-made material similar to the precious red stone. He coated both ends of the rod with a layer of silver that would reflect light.

Maiman then placed the rod inside the glass coils of a photographer's flashlamp. When the power was switched on, the light excited the atoms in the ruby rod, making them give off bursts of photons. The reflective silver coating made the photons bounce back and forth inside the rod, exciting other atoms. Light from all this activity was then allowed to escape through a small hole in the end of the rod. The light, millions of times brighter than sunlight, was more brilliant than any light that had ever been produced.

Soon after Maiman's experiment, other scientists began building different types of lasers by using rods made of

The space sail Starwisp would utilize microwaves instead of light waves to move it through space.

various materials. Although the types of lasers varied, the principle in each was the same: when certain atoms are excited by an energy source, they release the extra energy as light.

Modern lasers can create beams of light that are intense enough to bore holes through diamonds. Some lasers are being used to send radio and television signals and to guide satellites in space. A laser orbiting our Solar System could one day provide the light source to propel a sail toward distant stars.

Utilizing the New Technology

In 1984 Dr. Robert L. Forward of Hughes Research Laboratories designed a spaceship for interstellar travel. *Starwisp* would be a six-sided wire-mesh sail measuring 0.62 miles (1 km) across and weighing less than an ounce (28 g). Tiny microchips at each of approximately 10 trillion wire intersections would act as parts of a supercomputer system and also as pinhole cameras.

According to Forward's proposal, the sail would be built in space, somewhere beyond the orbit of Mars. After it was launched, it would be pushed by a beam from a **maser** (a laser that uses shorter waves, called microwaves, instead of light waves). The maser would be mounted on a satellite orbiting the Earth and focused on the sail by a special lens known as a Fresnel lens.

Pushed by the microwave beam, *Starwisp* would reach 20 percent of the speed of light in just one week. It could be three-quarters of the way to the Alpha Centauri system in 17 years. The microwave beam would then be aimed not at the sail but at the star system.

When *Starwisp* arrived in that area four years later, it would fly through the system, a distance of about 5.5 billion miles (9 billion km), in just 40 hours. It would pass through the microwave beam, which would supply the few watts of power needed to activate the spacecraft's microcircuits. The pinhole cameras would begin taking images and beaming them back to Earth. Four years later, when *Starwisp* would be almost one light-year past Alpha Centauri, its data would just be arriving back on Earth.

Another of Forward's designs, known as *Starlite*, involves a sail about three and a half times larger than *Starwisp*. The sail would be made of pure aluminum film and would carry a probe containing complex instruments. The probe would be used for gathering and sending back to Earth information about planets in other star systems that may contain some forms of life. The entire craft would weigh about 2,200 lbs (1,000 kg).

A laser three times more powerful than the maser and stationed on a solar-orbiting satellite would propel *Starlite*'s

Lasers would also be used to propel another advanced design that incorporates a large sail and a smaller one that acts as a decelerator, or brake.

Starwisp: *A maser-pushed interstellar probe.*

sail. The satellite would be located somewhere between the orbits of Saturn and Uranus. A Fresnel lens that was 600 miles (1,000 km) wide would focus the laser beam on the sail. *Starlite,* because of the size of its cargo, would be moving at only 11 percent the speed of light after 3 years. Even so, the craft would still reach the Alpha Centauri system within 40 years.

If evidence of life is discovered, an even larger craft could carry a crew to the star system for further exploration. This spacecraft would have three ring-shaped sails, one fitted inside the other. The smallest sail, measuring 62 miles (100 km) wide, would be the return vehicle. The next, a rendezvous sail, would be 200 miles (322 km) wide. The largest sail would be used as a decelerator, or brake, and would stretch 620 miles (1,000 km) across. The whole craft would weigh 842,000 pounds (about 381,900 kg).

A cluster of lasers would propel the vehicle to half the speed of light. In 20 years it could reach Epsilon Eridani, a star located 10.8 light-years from Earth. When it was less than a half light-year from its destination, the largest sail would be cut loose. The reflective surface of the remaining two-part sail would be turned toward the large sail. When light beamed from a laser located within our Solar System reached the decelerator, it would bounce back, striking the two-part sail from the opposite direction and gradually slowing it. The crew could then explore the star system.

After their work was completed, the crew would detach the rendezvous sail. A laser beam would strike that sail and bounce back, striking the return sail and returning it and the crew back to Earth. The entire trip would take about 51 years.

How could a crew survive such a long journey? Within the next century, technologies may become available that might make such a trip possible. Perhaps crew members might be placed in a state of **hibernation,** or even frozen. Or, maybe, the passage of time will one day be altered in ways we can now only imagine.

A space sail is shown in low Earth orbit (above) *and in a high Earth orbit* (facing page).

Conclusion

Scientists will continue to push for exploration of the far reaches of the universe. Hidden in other star systems and beyond them may be secrets that could provide tremendous insight into the origin of the universe. Toward these destinations solar sails may one day set forth.

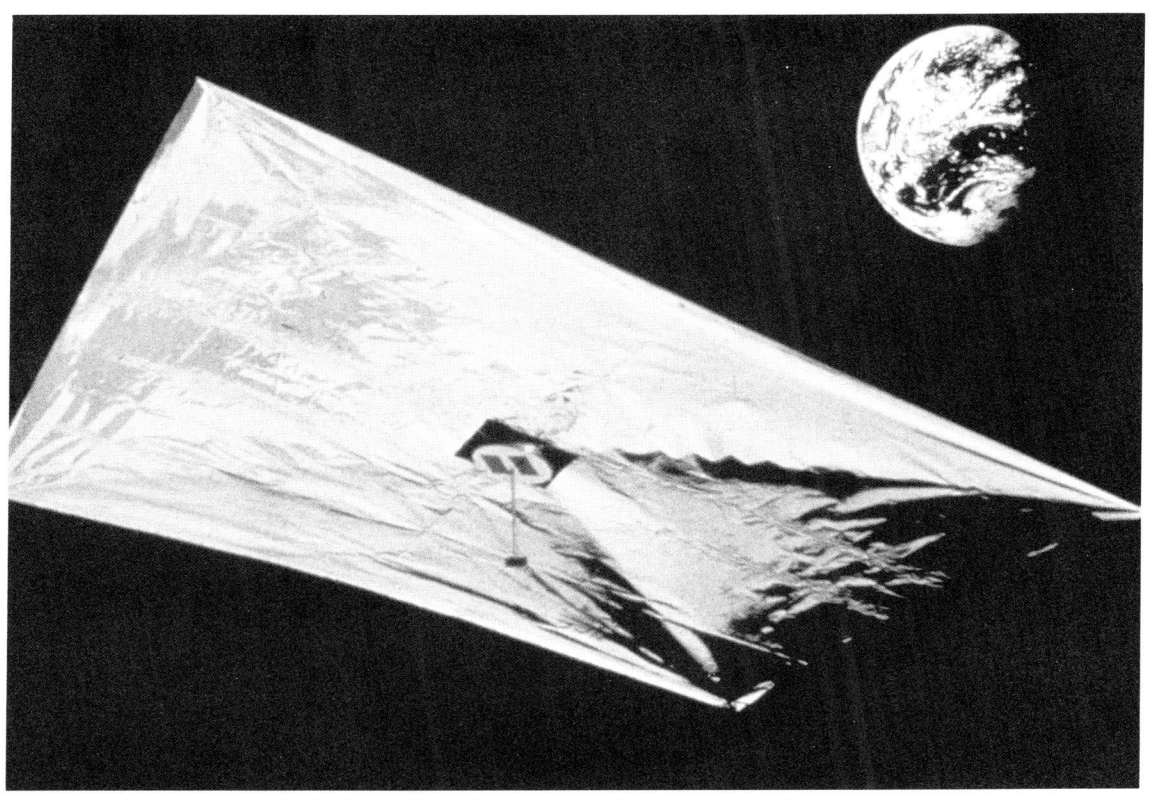

We can follow this dream, and so many others like it, if we only lift our heads and go!

—David Brin
Project Solar Sail

GLOSSARY

antimatter: material made of particles that have properties opposite to those of ordinary matter

axes: imaginary straight lines around which objects such as planets turn

centrifugal force: a force that pushes an object outward from its center of rotation

density: the amount of matter filling a space. If a space contains a very light substance, such as helium gas, the density of the matter in the space is low. If the same space is filled with a heavy substance, such as lead, the density is much greater.

escape velocity: the speed an object must reach in order to completely escape the pull of Earth's gravity

fusion: the joining of atomic nuclei to form heavier nuclei. During the process, huge amounts of energy can be released.

gravity assist: the use of a planet's gravity to sling a passing spacecraft into a different trajectory

hibernation: a resting state, in which a body's systems are slowed dramatically

laser: a device that produces a strong, narrow beam of light capable of traveling long distances without spreading out. The word *laser* stands for *l*ightwave *a*mplification by *s*timulated *e*mission of *r*adiation.

light-year: the distance that light, which moves at 186,300 miles (299,800 km) per second, travels in one year

maser: a device similar to a laser, except that it uses microwaves, rather than light waves

mass: the amount of matter in an object or a substance. On Earth, mass is the same as weight.

orbit: the path taken by a body, such as a planet, as it revolves around another body

photons: particles of energy that make up light

radar: a device that locates an object by analyzing the time it takes for radio waves to reach and be reflected by the object. The word *radar* stands for *radio detecting and ranging.*

rendezvous: matching the speed of a target and moving with it

space shuttle: a reusable spacecraft that can carry cargo, satellites, and passengers into space and bring them back

spar: a strong pole for supporting a sail

trajectories: the curved paths taken by spacecraft

vacuum: a space that has nothing at all in it, not even air

INDEX

photons, 8, 10, 15, 20, 25, 36, 45, 50
photon pressure, 10
Planetfest, 31
Progress M-15, 37
Project Daedalus, 50

radar, 43
rectangular sail, 20
Russia, 37. *See* Soviet Union

Sakigake spacecraft, 30
space sail fabrics. *See* aluminum, Kapton,
 Lexan, , Mylar, silver
space sail shapes. *See* disk, heliogyro, kite,
 rectangular, sunflower, triangular
Saturn, 31, 41, 45, 52
silver, 15
Skylab, 39
Solar Space Race Vehicle (SSRV), 36, 37, 43
Solar system, 17, 27, 29, 43, 44, 49, 52, 55
solar winds, 8, 17, 44
Soviet Union, 30, 33. See Russia
space shuttle, 24, 29
Spain, 33, 35, 36

square sail, 17, 20, 24, 31, 35, 43, 44
Starlite, 52, 55
Suisei spacecraft, 30
Sun, 8, 11, 15, 17, 25, 39, 43, 44, 45
sunflower sail, 35

triangular sail, 20, 35
Tsander, Fridrikh, 10, 13
Tsiolkovsky, Konstantin, 10, 13

Union Pour la Promotion de la Propulsion
 Photonique (U3P), 31, 33
United States, 7, 33, 35, 44
Uranus, 41, 52

vacuum, 10
Vega 1, *Vega 2* spacecraft, 30
Venus, 10, 41, 44, 45
Viking Mars lander, 24
Voyageur 2, 31, 41, 49

Wiley, Carl, 13
World Space Foundation (WSF), 31, 35, 36, 37
Wright, Jerome, 27, 29, 30

ACKNOWLEDGMENTS

The photographs and artwork in this book are reproduced through the courtesy of: pp. 2-3, Cambridge Consultants, Inc.; p. 6, NASA/Courtesy of The Planetary Society; p. 8, C.T. Thompson/Courtesy of Independent Picture Service; pp. 9, 18, 22, 23, 25, 40, 42, 43, NASA; pp. 11, 38, 60, Lunar & Planetary Institute; pp. 12, 19, 21, 32 (both), 56, 57, World Space Foundation; p. 14, The Johns Hopkins University/ Applied Physics Laboratory; p. 16, DuPont; pp. 26, 29, 30, 46, 48, 49,, 63, National Optical Astronomy Observatories; pp. 28, 36, European Space Agency; p. 34, Itar-Tass/Sovfoto; p. 41, 45, Space Studies Institute; p. 51, Hughes Aircraft Co.; pp. 53, 54, Dr. Robert Forward.
Cover photograph is courtesy of the World Space Foundation.

The author wishes to thank Emerson LaBombard and Stephen Brewster of the World Space Foundation, and Dr. Robert Forward for their assistance with this book.